KT-214-505

CHRISTMAS
The
Greatest
Gift

PAUL WILLIAMS

CHRISTMAS

The Greatest Gift

PAUL WILLIAMS

10 Publishing
a division of 10ofthose.com

First published in Great Britain in 2017

British Library Cataloguing in Publication Data
A record for this book is available from the British Library

ISBN: 978-1-911272-73-1

Designed and typeset by Pete Barnsley (CreativeHoot.com)

Printed in Denmark by Nørhaven

10Publishing, a division of 10ofthose.com
Unit C, Tomlinson Road, Leyland, PR25 2DY, England

Email: info@10ofthose.com
Website: www.10ofthose.com

Dedication

*In memory of Mum and Dad (Christine and Jack),
who gave me a love of Christmas.*

*With thanks to Caroline, who continues to make
every Christmas a special time with the family.*

Contents

INTRODUCTION:

Christmas Wrapping

I love Christmas. I love the food, the presents, time with the family, decorating the tree, singing carols – I love it all; well, almost all.

Almost, because there are some things about getting ready for Christmas for which I really don't care. I get frustrated when I can't find just the right present. I'm frustrated by the crowds in the shops. And I'm frustrated by sellotape! Yes, sellotape. It's essential for wrapping gifts. Arguably, it's difficult to get through Christmas without it. But sellotape is so utterly and annoyingly frustrating that it's enough to make you want to pull your hair out.

I reckon that, over the years, I must have wasted hours of my life looking for the end of the sellotape. When I do eventually find the end and think I can finally start wrapping presents, I peel back the sellotape only to find it rips diagonally towards the edge of the roll, leaving me with a small piece that is good for nothing. And I'm back searching for the end again.

With perseverance, I do eventually overcome the curse of the sellotape … until Christmas morning. Just when I think my annual battle with this sticky adversary is over, it turns out that an overzealous relative has used an entire roll of the stuff to wrap my gift, leaving me with the nigh on impossible task of getting into my present. At first, it's mildly amusing. Then annoying. And finally, it's embarrassing. The rest of the family are killing themselves laughing as they watch me struggle. I can't get into my present. I'm a grown man – I'm 55 years old – and I can't get through the sellotape.

Now I tell you about my struggles with sellotape for two reasons. First, it's cathartic to share it with you – I feel better already. But the second and main reason I share with you my seasonal frustration with sellotape is because, for many, the Christmas message feels a bit like that. You can't get into it.

Perhaps, over the years, you've met Christians who become very excited as they talk about the real meaning of Christmas and about a message of hope, joy and peace. You may even have heard some say that Christmas contains the most important message in the world, and you're intrigued. Maybe that's why you picked up this book. You may have a sneaking suspicion that, like sellotape, Christmas just might hold everything together. But you can't find your way into it.

In the pages that follow, I want to try to identify the sticking points and take off all the wrapping that surrounds Christmas, so you can get to the gift inside.

1

Surprise

I become very excited when I find the right Christmas present for the right person, especially when I know it's going to be a complete surprise. I've always loved surprises. The bigger, the better. When I was a kid, I used to get very excited when the biggest present under the tree had my name on it. Yet now that I'm a bit older – who am I kidding, I'm a lot older! – I've come to appreciate that it's sometimes the smallest presents that are the most surprising ... and expensive!

When a teenager unwraps their gift to discover there's a new smartphone inside, it's perhaps not the biggest present they'll receive, but it's probably the best and most costly. The smallest gifts often turn out to be the most valuable and the most thrilling of all.

And that's certainly true of Christmas, once we get the wrapping off and begin to see what it's really all about. The Christmas story is focused on the arrival of a very small 'package', a tiny, newborn baby:

[Mary] gave birth to her firstborn, a son. She wrapped him in cloths and placed him in a manger, because there was no room for them in the inn (Luke 2:7).

That's how Luke, one of the Bible writers, records the events of the first Christmas. Even if you have never read Luke's account of Jesus' life, I imagine you might well have seen the story acted out at a school nativity play. You might even have been one of the main characters and worn a tea towel on your head!

As with small presents under the Christmas tree, it turns out that there is much more to that tiny, human 'package' in the manger than you and I might first imagine. What we discover is very surprising indeed.

Another Bible writer, John, takes us right back to the beginning of time to help us grasp the amazing surprise hidden in the arrival of Mary's baby. John begins his account of Jesus by telling us some extraordinary facts about the person who would be born in Bethlehem. Referring to Jesus as 'the Word', John writes:

In the beginning was the Word, and the Word was with God, and the Word was God. He was with God in the beginning. Through him all things were made; without him nothing was made that has been made (John 1:1–3).

And John, who knew Jesus personally, adds a bit later:

The Word became flesh and made his dwelling among us. We have seen his glory, the glory of the One and Only, who came from the Father, full of grace and truth (John 1:14).

John is telling us two remarkable facts here. First, that this one he calls 'the Word' is actually God himself, the Creator of the universe. Second, that this person 'became flesh' – he became real flesh and blood. He was a human being. And he lived among us, here on planet Earth. So the great surprise of Christmas is that when you peep into the manger and look at the baby, you are looking at God.

Some years back, I heard about a primary school teacher who went into school towards the end of term feeling tired, lacking inspiration and without a lesson plan. 'This morning, class, we're going to do some painting,' she said. 'So get your aprons on and the paints out and begin painting. You can paint anything,' she continued, 'anything at all.'

So the class began. After a while, the teacher walked around the classroom, looking at their creations. There were pictures of Mum and Dad and the dog in the park. Others painted scenes on the beach. But the teacher was surprised when she came to six-year-old Scott's effort. The paper was just a mass of colours.

'That's very nice, Scott' said the teacher. 'What is it?!'

'Oh, that's God,' replied Scott.

'But no-one's ever seen God,' said the teacher.

To this Scott replied, 'They have now.'

No-one's ever seen God … they have now:

that's the big surprise of Christmas. It's mind-blowing. And it's exactly what the Bible writer John says:

> No-one has ever seen God, but God the One
> and Only, who is at the Father's side, has made
> him known (John 1:18).

Do you want to know what God is like? John says that, from the first Christmas onwards, you can know God like never before because he has come to earth in the person of Jesus. Incredibly, Christmas tells us that God can be known.

This is a huge claim. So how do we know it's true? Where's the proof? Extraordinary claims demand extraordinary evidence. We find such proof in the historical accounts of Jesus' life recorded in the Bible.

The Christmas story itself is full of 'out of the ordinary' events: a miraculous pregnancy; angels announcing Jesus' birth; a star guiding wise men to worship Jesus. This was no normal birth.

But there's more – much more – because the baby grew up. As Jesus walked this planet, he did amazing things, astonishing things, things that only God could do.

In the rest of his book, John records some of Jesus' miracles. Jesus turned water into wine; he healed a boy who was close to death; he enabled a cripple to walk again; he fed more than 5000 people with a little boy's sandwiches; he walked on water; he gave sight to a blind man. Jesus even raised a man from the dead. Jesus did things that are out of this world to prove that he was from out of this world.

Recently, I talked to a man called Jim who was very sceptical about the miracles of Jesus. So I asked him, 'If someone were to walk into the room right now and say, "I'm God!" what would you say?'

Quick as a flash, Jim replied, 'I'd say: prove it.'

I responded, 'That's exactly the point, Jim. If someone claimed to be God but couldn't do anything extraordinary, you wouldn't believe they were God and nor would I.'

The miracles of Jesus are exactly the reason to believe that he is God. They are precisely what we'd expect God to do while walking this planet.

Bertrand Russell, the atheistic philosopher, was once asked what he would do if, when he died, he discovered that God was there after all. He said, 'I would ask God why he hadn't given more evidence for his existence.' Bertrand Russell laid the blame for his unbelief firmly at God's door.

Many people feel the same. They state, 'It's not my fault that I don't believe. If God is really that clever, that big and that powerful, why doesn't he show himself to me?'

Yet the great surprise of Christmas is this: that is exactly what God did in the extraordinary events that began in Bethlehem 2000 years ago. He made himself known.

At Christmas we see a baby who is God. We discover a very small 'package' containing the Creator of the world. That is a surprise! But it's more than that – it's wonderful news. It means that we can know for certain that God exists. So when it comes to knowing God, we're not left in the dark any more.

2

Lights

By now, it will be obvious to you that I love Christmas. One of the many things I love at Christmastime are the lights. Through the dark, cold, winter nights, it's brilliant seeing bright, coloured, flashing lights brightening up the place – in the city centre, in shops, in gardens and, of course, on Christmas trees. I love Christmas tree lights. At least, I love them once they're up and working.

What is it about Christmas tree lights? Every year, when I get them out of the box, they're always in a mess. When I pack them away at the start of January, I lay them carefully in the box so they won't get tangled. But every December, without fail, I unpack the Christmas lights only to find them tangled up. All they've done is sit in the loft for 11 months, so how do they get themselves into such a twisted, messy muddle?

Anyway, I manage to carefully unscramble them and lay them out on the living-room floor. But then when I plug them in, they don't work. What is that about? They were working the previous year, when I carefully put them away in the box. How can they not work now, when all they've done is sit in a box in the loft?

All that said, I still love Christmas lights – once they're untangled, working and on the Christmas tree. And I love them not just because they brighten up cold, dark nights, but because they represent something amazing.

In John's Gospel, Jesus is described as 'the light'. John writes:

'The light shines in the darkness, but the darkness has not overcome it' (John 1:5).[1]

Twice in my life, I have been in complete and utter darkness. The first occasion was on a guided tour of a cavern. Deep down in the cave,

---

[1] See the NIV footnote for this translation.

the guide switched the lights off. It was so dark I could not see my hand in front of my face. It was a very unnerving experience.

The other time I was completely in the dark was when I was working for what used to be called the Midland Bank. But working for the bank is not the dark experience I'm thinking about, although it wasn't a barrel of laughs! No, the darkness I'm thinking of occurred one day in the week before Christmas when I had to go with a colleague to a huge, underground warehouse where millions of documents were catalogued and stored. Our task was simple: to locate a few dockets. While we were there, the lights went out. My colleague and I found ourselves in a vast, subterranean warehouse with not a shaft of light from anywhere. This was long before the days of mobile phones, so we didn't have any source of light to hand and we couldn't make a call to tell anyone what had happened. As I stood there, I could see nothing – not a thing. And even though I didn't move, I soon found myself disorientated and quite fearful. It was horrible.

Whether you've had that kind of experience or not, most of us know what it is to be in the dark: during a power cut, or at night when the main fuse blows in the house, or walking down a road without any street lights. Darkness, and even the thought of being in darkness, evokes all sorts of negative emotions: uncertainty, confusion, a sense of being lost and, of course, fear.

Light, on the other hand, brings confidence and reassurance, and makes us feel safe. As soon as the lights come on, we can see where we're going. This is exactly why Jesus is described as 'the light'. Indeed, Jesus called himself 'the light of the world' (John 8:12 and 9:5). Knowing Jesus gives us safety and security, and shows us where we're going in life. And knowing what life is all about is a brilliant thing.

A few years back, the church I'm part of put to family, friends, colleagues and neighbours the following: 'If you could ask God one question and you knew it would be answered, what would it be?'

I asked that same question to a bloke called Martin and he said, 'If I could ask God one question, I'd ask him, "Is Elvis dead?"'

I replied, 'That would be your one question for God?'

'Yes,' said Martin.

I commented, 'That's hardly a matter of life and death.'

To this Martin replied, 'It is if you're Elvis.'

Fair point!

Anyway, when all the hundreds of replies came back to us, it turned out that one of the most asked questions was, 'What's the meaning of life?' Now that says something.

Here we are on this little, blue–green planet, hurtling through space and circling the sun at around 67,000 miles an hour. But many of us – and if our survey is anything to go by, it seems most of us – don't know why we're here, or what on earth it's all about. We're wandering through life in the dark, trying our best to make something of life, but being in the dark makes living life, raising a family and making decisions very difficult. This is why the message of Christmas is brilliant. Jesus, the light of the world, has come into the world to make sense of the world.

Every year, at Christmastime, I have an overwhelming sense of not knowing where I'm going or for what I'm aiming. It happens when

I go Christmas shopping at our local shopping mall! All year round, I avoid the place like the plague. Therefore, when I do finally head there, I don't have a clue where anything is. So I wander around aimlessly, uncertain of what direction to go or what to buy.

My experience of Christmas shopping illustrates perfectly how life is for many people. We're wandering around, not really sure if we're going in the right direction or what we're looking for anyway. That is frustrating when it comes to Christmas shopping, but it's tragic when it describes our life because, let's face it, we only have one shot at life. So knowing what it's all about really matters.

That's why Christmas is so wonderful. It tells us that we can know the purpose of life because Jesus, the light of the world, has come into the world.

What exactly is life all about, then? That's what we'll explore next.

3

Food

Every Christmas I eat too much. I eat too many mince pies in the lead-up to Christmas. I eat too much chocolate right through Christmas. But my overeating reaches its excessive climax at lunchtime on Christmas Day.

For Christmas lunch I have everything there is going. Everything – with all the trimmings. At no other time of the year do I try to cram so much onto my plate and then attempt to eat it all. And then, when I'm finished, I have seconds … and then pudding … and then seconds of pudding!

At Christmas lunch, I eat a gargantuan amount of food in one sitting. And by the end of the meal, I regret it. I feel so full I can barely stagger to the sink to do the washing up. After clearing up the dishes, I collapse on the sofa to watch the Queen's Christmas Message, still feeling completely stuffed.

Next, it's time to unwrap our presents. Then my wife says, 'Anyone fancy something to eat?' Lo and behold, I find that I do. Just hours after consuming a gut-stretching lunch, I find myself tucking into a turkey sandwich and a piece of Christmas cake.

That perfectly illustrates an experience that is known by every human being who has ever lived. We all have an insatiable appetite – not just for food, but for life itself. We keep wanting more.

Barry Humphries, who is better known as Dame Edna Everage, opens his autobiography with these words:

I always wanted more. I never had enough milk or money or socks or sex or holidays or first editions or solitude or gramophone records or free meals or real friends or guiltless pleasure or neckties or applause or unquestioning love or persimmons. Of course, I have had more than my share of

*most of these commodities but it always left
me with a vague feeling of unfulfilment.*[2]

What Humphries expresses so clearly is what
we all know to be true in life, to a greater or
lesser extent. It seems no matter how much we
have, we can't keep our appetites satisfied. If we
take delivery of a new car, or buy new clothes,
or get a new gadget, for a while – sometimes
for months – we feel delighted with our new
acquisition Then, gradually, our hunger returns
and we begin to crave another one.

Likewise, we work hard to get a job or a
promotion. When we do, we're on cloud nine –
walking on air. But as time goes by, the elation
fades and we want more. We are not satisfied until
we've climbed the next rung on the career ladder.

What is true of acquiring possessions and
succeeding in our work can even be true in our
relationships. When we first met our significant
other, it was enough just to be with them, in their
arms, gazing into their eyes. Absolutely nothing
else mattered but to be in their presence. But

---

[2] Barry Humphries, *More Please* (Penguin, 2017).

then we find ourselves dissatisfied with the one we promised to be faithful to for the rest of our life. And another catches our eye and might even grab our heart.

C.S. Lewis makes the point that when we take a good honest look at ourselves, we know that deep down, we really want something that we cannot find in this world. He explains that there are many things in this world that promise to give us what we want deep down, but they never live up to their promise. He points to those feelings we have when we first fall in love, or visit a foreign country, or start a new area of study, but he says no marriage, no travel, no study will ever really satisfy us.[3] If C.S. Lewis is right, it's because we were made for something outside of this world.

Jesus Christ is that one from outside of this world, as we considered in chapter one. Listen to how he speaks into the never-fulfilling frustration of life:

---

[3] C.S. Lewis, *Mere Christianity* (first published by Geoffrey Bles, 1952).

I am the bread of life. He who comes to me will never go hungry, and he who believes in me will never be thirsty (John 6:35).

It's a remarkable claim. Just as a good meal satisfies our physical hunger, Jesus says he can satisfy our appetite for life permanently. Where nothing in this life satisfies us for long, Jesus says he can satisfy us forever. He promises that those who come to him and believe in him will never again experience that deep inner yearning for something more.

Jesus is so confident that he is what we're looking for that he urges us not to look anywhere else for that missing ingredient in life. He says:

Do not work for food that spoils, but for food that endures to eternal life, which the Son of Man will give you (John 6:27).

The 'Son of Man' is a favourite title that Jesus used to describe himself. His claim is to be able to give us a quality and quantity of life that will never leave us wanting more.

When we get to know Jesus, we can begin to have that deep-down satisfaction now as we look forward to eternity in a new world that is perfect. And how we need that future eternal life, because life now is so very far from perfect.

4

Christmas Ruined

As if Christmas shopping isn't frustrating
enough, the whole retail experience is made
even more challenging by the music that's
piped through stores at Christmas. If it's not
Noddy Holder shouting, 'It's Christmas', then
it's some crooner 'singing' (and I use that word
advisedly) a cheesy melody. So as you wander
through the men's department looking for a
pair of festive socks for your uncle, you're likely
to hear Andy Williams warbling lyrics that tell
you, 'It's the most wonderful time of the year
… It's the happiest season of all'. It sounds good
(the sentiment, not the singing!), but many
who hear those words are desperately cringing.
And not just because they're trapped in a
department store listening to Andy Williams,

but because, for them, Christmas is a deeply unhappy experience.

Gingerbread, the single-parent charity, reports that the number of calls to their advice line, dealing with family breakdown, doubles immediately after Christmas. For many families, Christmas brings stress and debt. When a huge quantity of alcohol is added into that mix, you have a poisonous cocktail.

Domestic abuse and family disintegration are the extreme end of Christmas being ruined. But a family doesn't need to come anywhere near completely falling apart over Christmas for there to be a sense of relief when the in-laws finally get in their car to drive home!

A survey in 2010 revealed that 18% of people agreed with the statement 'I dread Christmas'. That's nearly one in five of everyone asked. A MORI Poll a few years back revealed that three million family rows take place in the UK over Christmas. Many of them begin over the smallest things. For example, Billy throws a wobbly when he loses at tiddlywinks, and as he goes into meltdown, he singlehandedly ruins Christmas for everyone else. What, moments earlier, had been a fun time playing family games, has been spoilt. You can make excuses for Billy: he's tired; he's overexcited; it's past his bedtime; he's only 18! But whatever defence you make, the truth is that he's just wrecked a perfectly happy moment. We get upset over the smallest things.

What happens at Christmas, happens all year round. Life is littered with disappointments and arguments. Then, when things don't go our way, we get grumpy and irritated with others. When life doesn't work out perfectly for us, we 'lose it' and take it out on others – often those closest to us. Why do we hurt the ones we love the most?

We need a bit of honesty here, because we are very good at projecting ourselves in a too favourable light. Many of the Christmas cards I am sent come with Christmas newsletters tucked inside. You know the sort of letters I mean: those with updates on the family, detailing what's happened since last year. They speak of exotic holidays, significant career advancement and the remarkable successes of the children. Here's an example:

Robert is doing brilliantly at school. Last year he took four GCSEs early and got A*s in them all. This year he'll take the rest of his GCSEs and his predicted A* grades across the board means he's aiming for Oxbridge as he begins studying six A levels next year. In sport, Robert plays tennis for the county, and we're in discussions with Manchester United Football Club who are trying to get him to sign for their academy. Robert has just taken his grade 8 cello, and we are told he also has a bright future as a concert pianist. Next week, we have a birthday party for Robert, when he will turn 12!

But here's the Christmas newsletter I've never received:

Susie got really disappointing grades in her GCSEs – because she's a lazy good-for-nothing who doesn't work hard and wastes hours on social media. Henry's no better – we can't get him off computer games and he's the grumpiest child you are ever likely to meet. I hate my job and frankly life is humdrum with nothing much to look forward to. Happy Christmas!

It's fascinating how we portray our lives in Christmas newsletters. We love to present the best side of ourselves. I do. Most people only see the acceptable face of Paul Williams. But there's stuff that goes on in my mind that is horrible. There are the thoughts I've had when someone has treated me badly. Then there are the things I daydream about that are far from edifying. And I'm yet to mention the grumpy, bad-tempered moments that no-one sees, except my poor long-suffering family. Our lives are far from perfect, but many of us become brilliant at hiding the darker side of our personality.

But while most of us can keep the lid on the ugliness in our lives, most of the time, and while we can fool other people, we can't fool God. He knows the truth that we've hurt others, been selfish and broken his rules. Worst of all, we ignore and reject God himself. That's the uncomfortable truth of the Christmas story.

John wrote these words at the beginning of his account about Jesus' life:

He was in the world, and though the world was made through him, the world did not recognise him. He came to that which was his own, but his own did not receive him (John 1:10–11).

Jesus – the one from outside of this world and the one who made this world – came into this world, but the human race didn't want him in their world. Humanity didn't acknowledge Jesus as God. His own people didn't receive him. They put him on a cross.

That is what happened back then, when Jesus walked this earth, but it still happens today. We don't recognise his authority to tell us how to live and we don't like it when he does. This is what the Bible calls sin. And sin not only ruins Christmas and the rest of life, but it leaves us in a very precarious position. For one day we will die and the Bible tells us that after death we will face God as our judge – the very God we have largely ignored and rejected all our lives. We need help.

So when we read that an angel announced to shepherds that a 'Saviour' had been born in Bethlehem (Luke 2:11), that's very good news indeed. A Saviour, a rescuer, is exactly what we need! We are in need of someone to save us from the very serious problem of having pushed God out of our lives.

What blows my mind is that the very God we reject came and rescued us at great cost to himself – all because he loves us.

5

Christmas with Love

In the lead-up to Christmas, I find myself writing two words over and over. As I wrap presents and then stick on a label, I write, 'With love.' And I mean it. I'm saying, 'This gift comes with my love.'

The first Christmas was also an expression of love: God's love. We see this in John's Gospel with, arguably, the most famous words in the whole Bible. Jesus says:

> *God* so loved *the world that he gave his one and only Son (John 3:16, emphasis mine).*

Jesus' birth was the beginning of the greatest demonstration of the love of God that the world has ever seen. As we look at Jesus and what he accomplished through his earthly life and death, we are looking at the very heart of what Christmas means. Christmas is God saying, 'I love you.'

To express his immense love for us, God couldn't have given a more precious or valuable gift. God's gift to us was not chosen from a department store or ordered online. He gave us a unique gift: he gave His Son. And this gift is a gift we all need, whether we know it or not.

From the beginning of December, Caroline, my wife, repeatedly asks me what I want for Christmas. I am hopeless at giving her ideas. But on Christmas Day, as, one by one, I open my presents from Caroline, I think to myself, 'That's just what I wanted,' even though I didn't know I wanted some of those gifts.

Caroline knows me and she loves me. The gifts she gives me shows me that she knows me and that she loves me. That's how it is with God's gift to the world. Jesus continues:

God so loved the world that he gave his one and only Son, that whoever believes in him shall not perish but have eternal life (John 3:16).

As we considered in the last chapter, we have a problem. A really serious problem. Not only do we sometimes manage to ruin Christmas because of our selfishness but, and far more alarmingly, we have ruined our relationship with God. So the prospect of standing before God one day should terrify us. By rights we should be thrown out of God's presence forever – never enjoying the eternal life with him for which we were made; never experiencing the complete satisfaction for which we long; but rather being cut off from God forever.

John calls this perishing. That may sound like a word from a bygone era. We could imagine it being the word a news editor would select to describe the tragedy of the sinking of the Titanic over 100 years ago: '1517 souls perish as the Titanic sinks.'

But 'perish' is not written here in John's Gospel because it's an old-fashioned word. It is quite deliberately chosen as a word which describes a fate worse than death: being separated from God for all eternity. That's what we deserve because of our rejection of God. But it's not what God wants for us – because he loves us. And so he sent his Son, Jesus, in order that we might not perish but rather have eternal life.

Eternal life is brilliant. It's not just life that goes on forever and ever, but it is a quality of life. It is to experience and enjoy the life that we want deep down – a life that is deeply and fully satisfying and fulfilling all the time. It is a life of perfect paradise, when individuals will never want for anything.

God loves you so much that he wants you to have that life – life in a new creation with him. It's amazing love. God loves us so much, even though we are far from lovely.

It's easy to love people who are lovely. At Christmas, it's a delight to spend time with people we like. But God's love is different. He so loved the world – you and me – in all our ugliness. Though we often ignore him and shun him, and are thoroughly unlovely in our dealings with him, God so loved us that he gave his one and only Son – the most precious thing he has – to save us from perishing.

In fact, God sending his Son points us not only to the beginning of Jesus' life and the little baby in the manger, but also to the end of Jesus' life and the man dying on a cross – a cruel, painful, place of execution.

It is at the cross of Jesus that we see the full extent of God's love. It is at the cross of Jesus that we see exactly how we can be saved from perishing. On the cross, Jesus – who was perfect – took our place. Though he was without sin, he died for all *our* mistakes in life – especially for our rebellion against God. Wonderfully, the Bible also tells us that, as promised, Jesus rose back to life after three days, opening up the way for us to enjoy the same eternal life.

In the lead-up to Christmas last year, I heard on the radio a man talking about his gambling addiction. He'd taken out more and more loans to pay off his gambling debts, leaving himself with other huge debts he couldn't repay. He borrowed money from unscrupulous loan sharks – with ridiculous interest rates. They threatened that if he didn't pay up, he'd be beaten up. The radio interviewer asked him what he did. He replied, 'Thankfully, my family stepped in.' He explained how a member of his family went to meet the guys who had threatened him. But this family member took a beating for his troubles.

So, fearful of these brutes, the family member then remortgaged his house and paid off the loan.

It's not perfect as an example but that is a picture of something of what Jesus did as he died on a cross. He stood in our place. He took the beating – dying in our place. And in doing so he paid the price – clearing the debt of our sins. We should be rejected by God and perish for all the things we've said, thought and done that hurt others, not to mention the times we've pushed God out of our lives. But Jesus took our punishment. That's how much he loves us. Jesus' death means we can be forgiven and acceptable to God.

At Christmas, God gave us a wonderful gift – with love.

CHRISTMAS
The
Greatest
Gift
PAUL WILLIAMS

6

Unwanted Presents

It's great receiving presents, but I think it's even better giving them. Except every year, as Christmas Day approaches, I live with one fear – a fear that has been with me for more than 45 years now. It is the fear of giving an unwanted Christmas gift.

My fear goes back to when I was eight or nine years old and gave a present to a relation. In our house, we used to make a big deal of present giving. We'd all sit around in a big circle and hand out our presents one by one, with everyone watching while the gift was unwrapped. When my turn came, I gave my present to my relative. She took it and unwrapped it. It was a gift set of delicate lace handkerchiefs. She took one look at it. Then, in front of the rest of the family, she said to me, 'What would I want those for?' I was devastated. At the end of the day, when she set off home, she actually left them behind. She clearly didn't want my gift.

Having your gift rejected really hurts. And a rejected gift is the sad element of the Christmas story. John wrote of Jesus:

> He was in the world, and though the world was made through him, the world did not recognise him. He came to that which was his own, but his own did not receive him (John 1:10–11).

Being an unwanted Christmas present, tossed aside, was God's experience that first Christmas. God gave the world his most precious gift: his Son, the Lord Jesus. He gave us the gift we need more than anything. Yet the world rejected Jesus. They hung him on a Roman cross – the cruellest of executions. God, in Christ, came among us and we said, 'What would I want him for?'

But, as we've seen, the most unwanted yet most valuable Christmas gift of all is also the one we desperately need. John writes in

very clear and stark terms about the decision
before us all:

*He came to that which was his own, but his
own did not receive him. Yet to all who received
him, to those who believed in his name, he
gave the right to become children of God (John
1:11–12).*

We can receive the gift God gives us – his Son
Jesus – or reject him. To treat Jesus like an
unwanted gift is to reject God who gave the gift.

What's more, to reject God's gift is the most
costly mistake we can make because it is to
reject eternal life, the inheritance God gives to
his children. So don't reject Jesus. Don't look at
him and think to yourself, 'What would I want
him for?' Take the gift.

7

Taking God's Gift

You've made it to the last chapter. So I'm assuming you're still interested. I'm hoping that reaching this far means that you are getting through the Christmas wrapping and are able to see the gift at the heart of Christmas.

As a little boy, I used to get so excited about opening my Christmas presents. In fact, I was so excited that I'd wake up regularly throughout Christmas Eve night, creep into my parents' bedroom and whisper (loudly), 'Is it time to get up yet? Can we open the presents now?' This happened so many times throughout the night that when it was finally time to get up, my mum and dad were exhausted.

So one year they told me on 21 December that there were five sleeps until Christmas Day, when there were actually just four sleeps to go. That year I went to bed on Christmas Eve night thinking the next day would be Christmas Eve. In the morning, Christmas Day, I woke up at 7 a.m. to see presents at the bottom of the bed. I ran into my mum and dad's bedroom shouting, 'He's come early – Father Christmas has come early!'

These days I don't need to be duped into having a good night's sleep, but I'm still excited about getting presents. So it won't surprise you to know that once Christmas Day has come, I have never left a gift with my name on it, under the tree, unopened. Never.

But that's what thousands of people do with the gift that God has given. They never take the gift for themselves. I have met many people – and many of them actually go to church – who have never 'received' Jesus. But the good news is this:

> ... to all who received him, to those who believed in his name, he gave the right to become children of God (John 1:12).

It is only those who receive Jesus as their Saviour and believe in his name, trusting all he has accomplished for them on the cross, who will receive God's gift of becoming his child.

In the days leading up to Christmas, parcel deliveries come thick and fast. If you're out when the postman comes to your door, you'll find a little card on your doormat. It tells you that there is a parcel waiting for you back at the post office. And it will stay there until you take action. If you never go and ask for it, you will never receive it. You need to take it!

The same is true of God's gift to you. To have God's gift, you have to take it! And this is how you receive it:

- **Admit that you have sinned and rejected God.**

- **Believe that Jesus, the baby of the Christmas story, is God's one and only Son who came to us in human flesh.**

- **Believe that Jesus' death for you can bring you forgiveness and eternal life.**

- **Receive Jesus, asking him to be your Saviour.**

- **Receive Jesus into your life, acknowledging him as your Lord to direct your life, for the rest of your life.**

If, as you've read this little book, you've realised that you need Jesus and you are ready to receive him into your life, let me urge you to pray this prayer:

Lord God Almighty, thank you that you love me so much that you gave your Son Jesus at Christmas. I have come to realise that I have cut you out of my life. Please forgive me. Thank you that Jesus died so that I can be forgiven for all my sin.

I want to receive Jesus into my life, to direct my life, for the rest of my life. I want you to adopt me as your child, to know you as my heavenly Father and to be sure of eternal life with you forever. Please make me your own today. Amen.

If you pray that and mean it, then you can be sure that God will answer it. Through Jesus he will forgive you. By his Holy Spirit, Jesus will come and live in you. If you earnestly say that prayer, you will be a child of God. You can be sure that you will inherit eternal life. **It's 'the greatest gift'.**

If you have said the prayer on the previous page, you now need to know how to live with God as your heavenly Father and with Jesus as your Lord. I recommend you start by reading John's Gospel, which will tell you more about Jesus and what it means to follow him. If you write to me at: paul@thegreatestgift.org.uk I'd be delighted to send you a copy, and will also try to put you in touch with other Christians in your area who can help you as you begin your new life in Jesus.

Meanwhile, if you visit: www.thegreatestgift.org.uk, you'll find more about the true meaning of Christmas and how to follow Jesus Christ.

Publishing

a division of **10** **of those**.com

10Publishing is the publishing house of **10ofThose**. It is committed to producing quality Christian resources that are biblical and accessible.

www.10ofthose.com is our online retail arm selling thousands of quality books at discounted prices.

For information contact: **info@10ofthose.com** or check out our website: **www.10ofthose.com**